G000020035

Camping Cookbook

Mouth-Watering, Family-Fun Outdoor Recipes to Enjoy Nature While You Cook

MARLON WELCH

Table of Content

Introduction

Nowadays, camping can mean various things, such as pop-up tents or campers and simple tents. There are pleasant methods of appearing in the forests; there is nothing as real as an outdated form of camping and lying down in a sleeping bag and tent for a night or two. By far, one of the means of exploring spectacular scenery is camping. It's an ideal place to take a break from modern life and the full schedule. Often, you would not have reliable power and the internet, enabling you to detox, destress, and observe the beauty of nature easily.

Intrigued by the gurgling flames, one will gaze into the flames, watching as the flickering pieces of ash climb upward and disappear into the dark sky. The squeaking cricket noises and then waking up to the sound of wind chimes and the new air in the morning was nothing like deep sleep. For those who have never been camping before, falling asleep overnight in a tent in the middle of the woods may sound crazy. Yet, it will be a treat for those who enjoy Mother Nature and adventures.

Better still, camping is relatively cheap if you invest in the proper facilities. Camping requires just a tent, a sleeping pad, and maybe a minimal campsite charge, although many vacations come with lavish hotel and activity costs. If you are searching for a fast family escape on a budget, camping is an economic decision to consider. Instead of enjoying costly vacations overseas, you can save money and go on field trips to the places of your choice when you grow up. Although it may not sound as glamorous as a Disney World visit, for both adults and teenagers, there is a wonderful experience to be had in the natural environment. This is because of such camping trips that it is easy to generate passion and appreciation for nature, which everyone will benefit through.

You will get to know all the important stuff needed for camping in this book and how you can make your camping trip unforgettable with tasty recipes and fantastic food.

Chapter 1: Requirements for Camping

There's nothing quite like the experience of sitting around a campfire, grilling something with friends or relatives, and looking at the stars before cuddling in a cozy sleeping bag & being wooed to sleep by the symphony of nature. Camping is the best reminder that the most enjoyable might be the occasional simple and hard existence, whether you are wandering away from the city for a while or would want to reconnect with nature.

Although states are revived largely due to the recent Covid & domestic travel on the increase again after shutdowns, some people are still not yet prepared for a resort or holiday rented stay. Plus, after spending a lot of time indoors for the past few months, going outdoors and exploring wide-open spaces could sound exceptionally heavenly. For now, some may also feel better staying in their tent, where it is much easier to exercise social distancing than at a hotel. Instead of one of their canceled vacations this year, 47 percent of leisure travelers who choose to camp want to do so, as per the U.S. Survey in National Camping.

However, it is important to hold in mind that when it comes to flying, there is little guarantee of safety without a vaccine. And unless you plan to do wilderness camping and pack in anything you're going to use, there's a good likelihood you might need some public camping facilities. If you choose to camp outside your home state, it is necessary

to pursue the best practices of the CDC & WHO to try to read up on any travel ban in the state. Besides, be conscious that due to the wildfires, some campsites and areas may be closed for now.

If you're looking for some hiking to relax, suggest starting here with the best selection of campsites. However, with the growth in demand for camping, many campsites are filling up rapidly. And if you're ready to take your dogs with you, be sure to search the guides for dog hiking.

This list is an excellent starting point for car campers & tent-pitching newbies, but you'll need to make sure that you create your own special list based on certain key variables.

Next, remember how many others you're going for. If it's a family/friend camping trip, you'll want a four-person tent or two different tents, so adults and kids would both have different positions. If you are heading out for a solitary experience, a smaller 1-person tent suits just right.

1.1 Where are you on the road to camp?

Is it also a critical part of what kind of campsite you are going to or how long you plan to stay? Will you have running water at the campsite, or do you need to bring your own bottles of water? Is this off the main road or deeper into the wilderness where no cell service might be available?

You would want to take that into account when making decisions such as how extensive the first aid kit might be. It is therefore wise to schedule snacks and meals in advance to ensure that no matter how long you're away, your nutritional needs are fulfilled.

1.2 What do you intend to do?

In the end, don't forget to consider the stuff that you would want to see. If you're heading to a river anywhere, fishing is permitted. Carry in a fishing rod as well as a tackle box. Take a board game or other activities that are easily compact while camping with friends. If you schedule intense hiking, make sure you have route maps on hand and comfortable hiking footwear.

If that sounds daunting, please don't panic at all. With this comprehensive camping list, it will assist you in obtaining all the necessities.

To determine what gear you need to take on the journey, consider these three questions:

Are you planning to head to a primitive campsite or campground?

This will offer you a clearer understanding of whether or not there will be available picnic

tables, bathroom facilities, water, fire pits, and electricity. Clearly, you'll have to pack a little differently for primitive camping.

What things would you like to do?

You will assess if you'd prefer to spend your time outside. Complete the gear list with the stuff you need to make biking, hunting, biking, playing sports, or just relaxing at the camp fun.

How relaxed would you want your camp to be?

Think of your campsites like a blank canvas where you can set as much or as little as you like to create it. Some individuals take great pride in putting up large, cushy camps, while others take a minimalistic approach.

1.3 What's the weather forecast?

What you pack, the season and the situations also make a big difference. During warmer months, when lighter clothes and less heavy-duty boots are preferable, most casual campers typically go.

If you choose to camp in the winter or somewhere with snow, you'll want to add items like snow jackets, gaiters, & thermal gloves to the list. Packaging a spare blanket and an extra pair of socks does not hurt.

1.4 Starting from Scratch?

While this gear list can at first appear daunting, you can find that you have many of these items around the home. Start by first gathering the necessary necessities, then grow from there, such as your shelter & bedding. If you are on a limited budget, try renting / borrowing things to get underway. When you go for more holidays and learn to love camping, the camping equipment can be updated and modified.

CAMPING LIST

GENERAL
- Tent
- Tarp X 2
- Stakes
- Mallet/Hammer
- Folding Table
- Camping Chairs
- Canopy
- Clothes Line
- Clothes Pins
- Rope
- Lantern
- Flashlights
- Head Lamp
- Firewood
- Hatchet/Ax
- Lighter Fluid
- Gloves
- Lighter
- Plastic Bags
- Trash Bags
- Zip Ties
- Twine
- Bungie Cords
- Spade
- Toilet Paper
- Paper Towels
- Duct Tape
- Portable Fan
- Hand Warmers
- Bug Spray
- Personal Backpack or Camelback
- Rain Ponchos
- Beach Towel
- Check
- Water Jug
- Reusable Water Bottle
- Sunscreen

KITCHEN
- Cooler
- Ice
- Camping Stove
- BBQ
- Propane
- Napkins
- Paper Towels
- Cutting Board
- Frying Pan
- Pot
- Knives
- Forks
- Spoons
- Spatula
- Whisk
- Knife Sharpener
- Wooden Spoon
- Tongs
- Skewers
- Scissors
- Roasting Stick
- Foil
- Can Opener
- Shoe Organizer
- Dish Soap
- Sponge

BAR
- Bottle Opener
- Cork Screw
- Cups
- Shot Glasses
- Cocktail Shaker
- Coffee Press
- Mugs

FOOD
- Spices
- Hot Sauce
- Salt/Pepper
- Condiments
- S'mores Kit
- Cooking Oil/ PAM
- Instant Coffee

SLEEP
- Sleeping Pad
- Sleeping Bag
- Pillows
- Blankets
- Eye Mask
- Ear Plugs

FIRST AID
- Band-Aids
- Hand Sanitizers
- Neosporin
- Aloe Vera
- Nail Clippers
- Tweezers

FUN
- Picnic Blanket
- Tapestry
- Outdoor Rug
- Portable Charger
- Aux Cords
- Chargers
- Solar Powered String Lights
- Solar Powered Speakers
- Ping Pong Ball
- Hammock
- Hammock Straps
- Camera

CLOTHING
- Tee Shirts
- Tank Tops
- Leggings
- Shorts
- Underwear
- Sports Bra
- Hoodie
- Jacket
- Socks
- Mittens
- Hiking Shoes
- Flip Flops
- Pajamas
- Swimsuit
- Sunglasses

TOILETRES
- Deodorant
- Lotion
- Eye Drops
- Toothpaste
- Toothbrush
- Floss
- Contacts
- Contact Solution
- Glassed
- Wet Wipes
- Travel Towel
- Chapstick
- Brush
- Hair Ties
- Bobby Pins
- Dry Shampoo
- Feminine Products

Chapter 2: Beginners' Camping

Camping is an ideal place to experience the great outdoors, enjoy some fresh air, and share with friends and relatives a memorable time. Camping for beginners and novices can be tricky, but here are some of our best tips to make your first time camping pleasant and stress-free.

2.1 Picking your campsite

There would be a wide range of campsites appropriate for you for your 1st time camping. Things to look out for include whether or not they are labeled 'kid-safe' if pets are allowed, and facilities such as showers and toilets are available. It's a great decision to book a campsite with high-quality facilities and a surrounding town, as a novice camper, because if you miss something, there would be plenty of nearby restaurants and buy supplies.

Purchasing tents

Tents come in multiple sizes and shapes, and it's important to choose one that's right for you. When buying a camp, it's smart to choose a size or two larger than the number of people using it. This allows ample space for the equipment to be packed in the tent and provides a nice sleeping space.

Practice pitching your tent

Getting a tent to practice pitch at home is one of the most relevant suggestions for first-time camping. This would mean that you know how to set up and pack the tent, and any problems can be resolved when you are at the house, not at the campsite.

Have a practice camp

After you've got the tent practice pitch, why not hold a practice camp? Camping can be intimidating for starters, but experiencing a night in the back garden can help you determine the number of layers you need to carry and whether the equipment is suitable.

Create a Camping Essentials list

Camping for beginners, especially when you are not sure of the type of equipment you need, can be challenging. To ensure that none is left behind, check out our outdoor equipment guide for assistance, and develop your checklist.

Creation of Campsite

When setting up the tent and free of any obstacles that may harm your tent, try to pitch it in such an environment where the ground is flat, always bring the tent back to the wind to give it more balance, and place the pegs in the soil at a 45 ° angle.

Schedule the meals ahead

It will save a great deal of time and trouble for a novice camper to plan what you will eat & how you will prepare it. Review the campsite rules and see if campfires are allowed, and check for any restaurants or cafes in the surrounding area where you can eat if things don't go according to schedule.

If you get it right, camping for beginners can be enjoyable and memorable. Follow these tips, and on your very first camping trip, you are guaranteed to be a hit.

2.2 Wellness advantages from camping

There are a variety of good explanations for moving outside, but here's one you may not know: your well-being. The health benefits of camping and exploring nature are very well-documented, & if you need tension relief and a refresh, a good way to make it happen is to grab the tent and go out for an adventure. By camping, your mood, intellect, metabolism, and sleep habits will be enhanced, so look for a place, schedule your camping holiday and get on the road.

1. Enjoy the green space of the brain.

Curious why camping is fun for you? One of the great advantages being proximity to open space, as well as the natural world. Studies have shown that better and happier people are whether they enjoy time in nature or have plants around them, whether it's a glimpse of the park from their workplace or a regular trip through the trees. Scientists agree that our brains adapt to social views and exposure in age-old ways that positively affect mental well-being. Spending time with nature can increase the mood and help

you gain insight into life, particularly if it's for a couple of nights. If you are a nature lover, consider exploring any places popular for wildflowers in the summer, or consider planning a hiking trip to the Peak Area, the Lake District, or any location renowned for country walks and beautiful wildlife.

2. More workout than you get

A productive pastime is hiking. As you paddle, walk, or take a ramble around the countryside, you are increasing your physical activity rate and reaping many health benefits. More physical activity is required for a healthy heart, greater metabolism, and even more robust joints and muscles. Many of us don't get enough regular exercise because of the sedentary aspect of our work, and let's face it. It's a lot more enjoyable to go hiking around a natural forest than running on a treadmill.

3. Resetting the clock for the body

Research has found that waking up with natural light in the morning is a crucial element in resetting the body clocks to help us get better sleep. Our body clocks are a fundamental aspect of our well-being; scientists also realize that every cell holds messages about the correct time to sleep and wake up. The so-called 'circadian patterns' that jet lag/other variables interrupt and may have long-term health effects.

There is a higher likelihood of respiratory issues & immune system disorders than much of the population of polls with shift workers seeing circadian cycles all over the location. Getting up with the sun may sound odd if you are used to an alarm clock, but it has been shown to have some major advantages; it is worth trying to keep up with the same plan right when you go home, with an alarm clock or open blinds simulating natural dawn light.

4. You get more exposure to vitamin D

Vitamin D is important for the health of the bones and other aspects of our physical well-being, including our attitude. Our optimal amounts of it need to be maintained with at least 10 minutes of sunlight per day. The body is unable to produce vitamin D on its own and needs foods high in vitamin D and sun to be able to produce it, and that's why a bit of sun is a good thing every day.

5. You sleep better

There are a few aspects that will enhance the consistency of your sleep when camping. For example, you are unplugged from modernity because there is less willingness to stay up all night to watch box sets. On the other hand, you are less likely to have electronic devices that generate digital or "blue" light, which has been found to interfere with good sleep. You are still free from city disturbances and noise from the traffic. Owls & river noises, the relentless stream of honking horns and screaming crowds may be heard, however.

6. Social time is extended by camping

Camping is a shared practice that produces fun interactions, teaches children self-reliance and a greater appreciation of the natural world, and provides you with a dose of social contact that enhances your bonds, whether you are camping as a family or interacting with peers.

Campsites are often also sharing areas for people who express outdoor excitement, trade thoughts and inspire each other to invest some time. If you think you're lonely in the wilderness, all you'll have to do is walk away softly; nature is still there to be enjoyed.

The health benefits of camping are only one group of excuses to group out on your next adventure with your closest buddies.

7. Enjoyment of the current moment

A number of research have been carried out in recent years on the effects of mindfulness, a type of therapy that requires remaining very aware and at the moment. Camping is a fantastic way to experience sensitivity and see if the patterns of mood and fear change. The weight of the foot on the field, the smell of plants and leaves, the comfort of the air after a long walk, the ache of the thighs, and so on: listen to the body and how it is experienced in the natural world.

The outcomes, studies have shown, are strongly positive and help you act more intentionally; you would be more conscious of what the body says to you instead of sitting mindlessly and therefore react to it with further emphasis.

Without even thinking about it, the easiest way to get some vitamin D boost is to be out

and outdoors because you will most likely be on a camping trip. Going for a walk or cycle ride, cooking breakfast outside, among other stuff, will quickly give you a top-up. On hot days, continue to use sunscreen when you are out.

2.3 General advantages of camping

Camping provides a full spectrum of benefits for all, old and young, that you and the family can appreciate while spending time outdoors:

1. Lack of alarm clocks: When did you go to bed late last night to wake up without the need for an alarm clock? The sun and the chirping of birds are the alarm clocks you have while you are camping. Waking up with nature instead of an alarm clock is an opportunity that anyone should have.

2. Relationship building: One of the best and most significant aspects of camping is the way it lets you establish and strengthen relationships. When you go camping with family or colleagues, you have a chance to talk and communicate without interruption, sometimes late in the evening.

3. Better Food: Food only sounds amazing when consumed outside. There's something you can't replicate about cooking food over some campfire, campsite BBQ, or in some Deluxe Cabin kitchen when you feed at home. Plus, over any open flames, nothing can match mores packed. Dream high before you head out and plan the right meal for the next camping trip.

4. Unplugging: Camping is a great location for anyone to unplug and step away from the computers. In the outdoors, you don't see computers, iPads, or TVs because there is so much more to do that doesn't require electronics.

5. Production of new abilities: You cannot help but acquire new things while camping. Everyone is going to help, and learning ideas are a great place to grow. You'll learn how shelters, tie knots, build flames, cook dinner, and more are set up. Such talents are valuable to have, but during our busy everyday lives, we don't really get a chance to develop.

Although the benefits of adult camping also apply to young people, there are a number

of benefits that are special to young campers.

6. Nature interaction: When you camp, you have the ability to be in touch with nature, encounter animals, and gaze at the stars away from the harsh lights of the big city. There's nothing quite like it. Make sure that both you & the family have the potential to connect with nature when you explore the different benefits of camping.

7. Educational opportunities: Camping time for children is an initiative spent in learning; this is one of the reasons that scouting programs are so relevant. They advocate children-centered camping events that learn new skills, such as cooking, fishing, climbing, knotting, and fire-starting, first aid, fitness, and much more.

8. Family acquaintances: Camping is beneficial for kids and their families and will help strengthen interactions between family members, sisters, and brothers, kids, and parents, and the list goes on. You will all come home feeling much happier as a group.

9. Production of belief: Increasingly becoming more independent and progressively believing their ability is important for children. One of the benefits of youth camping is that it allows them to gain independence in a healthy and supervised climate. Kids become more optimistic as they experience new things and get first-time experiences.

2.4 Cooking Suggestions for the camp

When completed well, those taste of foods satisfies more frequently than some of those marked at the camp. All in the old-fashioned way of cooking makes the entire experience fresh, from preparing menus to savoring the last slice. However, a real drawback is that it requires more time, stamina, and ingenuity to prepare at the camp than to produce food at home.

Cooking Techniques

Outdoor adventurers had a lot of tactics on their heads in the old years to use a campfire for cooking meals. Of necessity, some are more difficult than others. Many camping tours, for example, do not need a roasting spit to be produced (only if you are overzealous). As we explain a few of the best, most effective methods of camp cooking, follow the methods.

The most popular solution to campfire cooking has been the usage of direct heat. There are a variety of ways to it. The first, the trick of old boy scouts, is to personally fill the aluminum foil with food items and ignite coals. It requires regular review. It is very effective, however, for food items that require high heat. The second solution is to position a grill over the blaze and, like you would cook your meal, mostly in the backyard of your house. The heat produced by such a direction is slightly more direct. Cooking, however, would typically take a little longer.

For soups, noodles, and stews, you will also need the pans and pots mentioned below in the stock list. To fry them, only build a fire, then allow it down to the burning coals and put the pan or pot over them. The trick of this method regulates the quantity & intensity of hot coal since fire may quickly become unpredictable. The great news is that campsite cooking is as simple as using a kitchen stove once you have it down.

Supplies for Cooking

There are a few classics of food preparation that you shouldn't necessarily miss, regardless of what you want to train for the next camping trip. First and foremost, a package of matches and even a few lighter fluids. The rest prefer to cook at their campsite over the flames, and when you don't find a way to launch it, you are out of luck. The real basics are pots, a lightweight moderate to a large jar, a comparable size tub, aluminum foil, and mobile grating that we might position over a fireplace. This blend of cooking equipment could be used to manufacture just about whatsoever, from eggs and bacon to pasta and beans. Finally, don't forget the tongs and spatula. Pulling food out of a bare-handed fire is far from enjoyable.

Some Basic Suggestions

- Measure and fill components for each dish in zip lock containers. Mark all bags properly.

- Prepare stews, soups, curry, etc. Ice them and place them in the refrigerator.

- Heat it for an immediate meal again.

- Be attentive to the canisters of petrol. Keep standing at all stages. Hold it in a well-ventilated spot outdoors. Through putting soap liquid over all linkages, search their leaky locations. When it is not in service, you can turn it off.

- The large, thick aluminum foil should not be overlooked. There are several other uses in the camp for it.

- Until throwing over the flame, the soap was placed on the exterior of the pans and containers, encouraging washing and defending against fire damage and smoke.

- Before setting it in the refrigerator, let the food be frozen. Other eatable products tend to be held frozen and would thus last longer.

- During outdoor cooking, cover pots. Food is going to be finished quicker, and fuel is going to be saved. It also helps safeguard the diet against insects and soil.

- All items in the cooler must be packed in waterproof bins or cases.

- To stop unwanted visits from pets, keep food inside, or hang above floor stage.

- Add oil to the camp grill to keep food from sticking.

- Usage of fireproof cooking devices. Keep the handles protected from excessive heat and flames.

- Bottles of frozen juice allow some things to keep cold.

- Using instant or snack foods for fast meals.

- Using zip lock bags to store items such as soup, chili, gravy, etc. Freeze the bottle and then lower the bottle into the cooler. It will help to keep some food cool.

- Keep matches dry and scratch the point of the match; illuminate when necessary. Keep your matches in a tube that also has a waterproof feature.

- When you feed, put the pan with warm water on the flame so it will be ready for cleaning when you have done.

- To keep the soap secure at your camping site, please put it in a soap jar or hang it by a branch.

- To fix the cooler's leak, add molten paraffin wax inside and outside the leaky area.

- Pita bread works smoother and keeps in better shape while camping than standard type bread.

- Making the hamburgers creates a hole in the middle of the hamburger around the size of the finger; during grilling, the hole will close, but the heart will be fried like the sides.

- Bring energy-raising snacks during meals, such as granola bars, dried or dehydrated fruit, jerky beef, etc.

- The ice cooler is operated, and an iced drink is provided.

- With the juice and water, fill 2-liter bottles & milk jugs, then freeze.

- Using a separate refrigerator for drinks such that the food refrigerator does not open as much.

- Clean to flush the odors from your cooler with a blend of baking soda and tap water.

- Periodically reload your ice. Keep the product preserved at all times to avoid spoiling and contamination of the product.

- In the container, apply a very minute volume of powdered sugar to keep the marshmallows from sticking together. The branded marshmallows are much less likely to bind together.

- If you create a meal of so much salt, introduce the potato to the recipe and finish the cooking process. The excess salt will be absorbed by the potato.

- Consider authorizing a crockpot to be included. Plan and schedule dinner early before your workouts. It'll be set for dinner once you get back.

- Pre-chop components, such as onions, tomatoes, etc., at home, loaded in zip lock sacks. Pre-cook the chicken & freeze for quick meal preparation.

- Using the surplus vegetables and meat to cook breakfast omelets on the last day of camp. You may allow the use of nearly any ingredient in omelets. You don't have to take the leftovers around with you.

- Prefer margarine to "squeeze" rather than margarine to stick. In the bush, it's either better or better to use squeezed bottles. It is also ideal for cooler climates. When it gets too tough, put it inside a pan of hot water for a few minutes.

- Cook (either coal or wood) over charcoal. Coals, lacking smoke, deliver a heat that's far more consistent. In the end, stop the food from getting fried.

- Storing nutritional products in individual zip lock containers. Savings in space. It's almost able to pack. Such resalable may be used for garbage cans when empty.

- Dense aluminum foil bags cover the least room for easy cooking and simple cleaning and are suitable for mixing meats and vegetables.

- Use your pots as bowl combos to conserve room when packing the kitchen at the camp.

- Roast the meat when barbecuing chicken with no sauce, unless the sauce is half fried and then sealed. It's not going to hurt the beef, and it's going to make your meal tastier.

- Plastic water bottles are utilized as better dispensers for salad dressings, sauces, and oils.

- To have the charcoal parts prepared faster, use a charcoal chimney.

- Add a few soap drops with ample water to cover the bottom of the pan and bring it to a boil to easily clean the burnt food in the pan.

- Apply any ice cubes onto the aluminum foil packs to prevent them from serious burns to hold them moist.

- Using a cloth/suede work glove.

- Use a huge old teapot to overheat the cooking water, create pans, or create hot beverages.

- Try out the description of the various (homemade) fire initiator models.

- Use 2 to 4 large coffee cans occupied with water and sealed with aluminum foil as grate holders. When the meals are prepared, water gets hot for dishes and washing. Please place them in your reusable bags in order to keep them protected from other

- kinds of stuff.

- If you are actually into outdoor hiking, purchase airtight containers. Without oxygen, bacteria do not reproduce (as fast), and cold food goods look to keep getting nice inside the airtight bags and organize individual portions to unlock what you want or need. Since the containers are reusable, use them as your garbage. They are much smaller relative to cans. Ultimately, the sacks are thicker than other storage bags, reducing the smell of food if it is not eliminated.

- Place a thread into the tissue feature tubing. The ends of the rope are Tie's, and they use it for a picnic table.

Different types of home-made fire starters.

1. Invest if you are very into outdoor camping in airtight enclosed bins or packs. Without warmth, microbes do not develop easily, and foods that are cold tend to keep growing healthier. Organize meals for individuals in airtight containers so that you only view what you desire. Specific pieces defrost more easily than bigger ones for iced products. Since the containers are reusable, use them for your garbage. These are much lighter than cans. Eventually, the tanks are heavier than other storage containers, and if not removed, they may minimize the smell of the product.

2. Using 2-4 big water-filled coffee cans and cover them in thick aluminum foil as grill holders. When your food is cooked, water gets hot for washing or clean-up. Store them in their plastic bags to preserve contamination from other items. Fold the plastic storage containers, along with dishcloth or cleaner, etc.

Chapter 3: Kitchen Camp Organization

In this segment, we will briefly address the organization of the kitchen camp.

3.1 What's there to bring for camping?

Your relaxation and willingness to love your experience to the utmost degree would have a huge effect on how you plan for camping. When you have the wrong gear, you will have a miserable time.

Below, you can find the items needed for camping.

1. Paracord Bracelet for Evacuation

This agile little gadget is critical whenever you go into the woods. In comparison to the long 12-foot paracord, it has a compass, emergency bell, compact knife, and fire starter built-in. For either wrist width, it's also adjustable and really cheap. Without one around, we will never go hiking or camping.

2. Solar telephone charger for phones

You're not going to find several electrical sources in the natural world, after all. A solar adapter with a USB link will charge your camera, light, phone, or other devices by using the sun's electricity. This waterproof gadget is hooked to your backpack so that you can use it to catch sunshine when hiking.

3. Cubes for packaging

If you want to be able to easily locate things in your tent, bag, or vehicle, you'll want a set of premium packing boxes like these. You pulled out the cube where you stored your denim instead of looking through it all to see if there is one clean denim. This is a camping game-changer.

4. Chilly Pad's Relaxing Towel

A chilly pad is a lifesaver when struggling to stay calm in the blistering sun. All you have to do is soak the cloth, squeeze the excess water out, and then feel the air 30 degrees cooler around your body, face, & shoulders. Once you try it, you'll never go camping without it. It takes 3 to 4 hours, and then what you need to do is soak it up again, and it can begin to work its magic. And it costs almost nothing.

5. Tent

Choosing the right tent is essential. A good tent is absolutely immune to the weather and easy to build. The design and layout of the tent you chose will rely on the size and space that your team requires, but this is a sturdy and very well-ventilated model. It is also one of the most economical camps in the sector, and it will last for many years.

6. Bag of sleep

It will be much more fun to sleep beneath the moon and star if you are in a season-appropriate, waterproof sleeping bag. It is also outright dangerous to attempt to camp without one that will give you ample warmth. This one is robust, lightweight, and easy to clean-check the temperature requirements and expect to keep safe and comfortable.

7. Solar Lantern

This is especially relevant when prohibiting fire when the only outlets illuminating the way are the stars and the moon. A solar lantern is ideal since it is not required to change any battery or energy supply. My preference is a vibrant, simple to bring, and collapsible one,

plus it should be light enough to take with you and put in your tent for inside illumination.

8. Windproof Portable Umbrella

Nothing is worse without the requisite rain cover than getting stuck in a rainstorm while camping. But if you hold a quality travel umbrella that is weather-resistant, then you can be guaranteed to be covered no matter what the weather ends up looking like. One can weigh less than one pound, be ultra-lightweight, and come with a promise of a replacement.

9. Foot Blister Balm

When you camp, you will be on your feet all the time and will definitely do a little hike that adds extra tension to your heels. To avoid the pain of blistered feet, bring this awesome blister balm, and you're not going to have an issue. It drifts on effortlessly and lasts a whole day by avoiding the additional friction that causes blisters.

10. Camping Parachute

At the end of a long hike, there is nothing like lying in a hammock under a large shade oak. This hammock should be lightweight, compact, simple to clean, and quick-drying. All you have to do is to find the right plants, and you will be set up in no time.

11. Quality Cooler

The trickiest part of camping is deciding whether to prepare and how to stop your food from falling dead. Whether you bring a camping stove (or a fireplace on-site), bring burgers, hot dogs, or something else that you would like to barbecue for dinner. Bacon and yogurt or eggs and granola for breakfast are several good combinations. Ensure that you have with you spatulas and metal tongs and perishable stock food in a quality cooler packed with ice.

12. Filtered water bottle

It's so crucial to hold a good-quality, reusable, distilled water bottle while camping. You can refill it in the water spigots of your camping area without caring about how healthy the source is, so it removes 99.99 percent of the waterborne bacteria, which will otherwise

render you sick. You may also draw water from a river or stream safely right away.

13. Stove with gas

It is a convenient way of cooking meals to carry a gas stove, particularly if your campground does not have a barbecue. One is super inexpensive, simple to handle, lightweight, and built by Coleman from good-quality materials.

14. Wipes with Deodorant

When hiking, you won't be forced to wash as much as you do at home, and you'll inevitably get dirty and stinky. Instead of stressing that your campmates can smell your stink, carrying a few of these wipes. Taking them out while you're in your tent or toilet, and with one fast scrub, you'll be stink-free and refreshed.

15. First aid kit

A lot could be done wrong on a camping trip. Be vigilant for splinters, blisters, cuts, and other even worse blunders with a rather well-stocked first aid supply. Keep it in your bag so that you can pull it out in need of an emergency.

16. Spray for Bear

Black bears visit much of North America's finest picnic sites and national parks. Hence, while hiking, it is a no-brainer to carry bear spray. You'll still want to take bear-proof containers of your food so that a bear doesn't try to get into your vehicle or tent at night.

In comparison, records suggest that you may still be covered from mountain lions wandering much of the same bear range through the bear spray.

17. Daypack for Hydration

It is important to remain organized with a sturdy daypack that won't harm your back. This one by Camelbak is amazingly well made for day hiking if you would rather be minimalist and just carry the water you need. It is super lightweight and weighs 50 oz., which is enough to hold you hydrated for a few hours.

3.2 What pots or pans for camping are suitable?

Backpackers, who make short trips or want simple, hardly any-fuss meals, maybe as little as a Spork and a cup, can need common cookware. Usually, more sections are required for campers, larger groups, and longer trips.

This section provides you with a review of your outdoor kitchenware options.

Specific cooking sets or pieces?

It is possible to buy a total range of cookware or cookware items bit by bit.

Cooking sets are ranges intended to bring the pots, pans, and lids together. Some cooking sets contain extras, such as plates, mugs, or cups that nest inside the containers.

Individual components help you to design your set almost the way you want it. This strategy may not be sufficient if you're trying to conserve weight for commuting and backpacking. It's a smart way to integrate versatility into your cookware range, however.

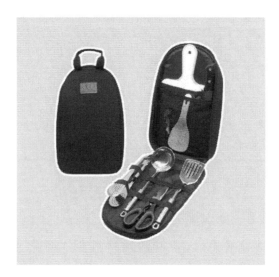

Cookware Material Options

1. Aluminum

Pros: Inexpensive, lightweight, and a great conductor of heat. Nice for bubbling foods without scorching.

Cons: When exposed to acidic foods, it tends to break down slowly.

2. Hard Aluminum

Pros: This form of material is oxidized and is long-lasting, and removes scratching and abrasion.

Cons: Nil.

3. Steel

Pros: Stronger, more resistant than aluminum to scratching.

Cons: Heat does not conduct as consistently, heavier than aluminum (may allow hot spots to scorch food).

4. Titanium

Pros: Incredibly lightweight, it is your lightest choice without compromising strength. Extremely corrosion resistant quickly heats up and performs effectively without full heat.

Cons: More expensive relative to other options. This brings out less consistent heat than stainless steel. To keep it from overheating, take caution.

5. Cast Iron

Pros: It is perfect and tough for frying or baking.

Cons: Quite heavy, not really for apps for backpacking. The right care is provided.

6. Non-stick (accessible on a few metal cookware) coatings

Pros: Sustain a clean breeze.

Cons: Less durable than regular surfaces constructed of metal. Some may be scratched with metal utensils.

7. Plastic

Pros: Non-abrasive, inexpensive, lightweight. Good for containers with utensils and airtight foods.

Cons: Not nearly as heat-tolerant or robust as metal. Many plastics can pick up and retain food odors or flavors.

Cookware Protection Concerns

1. Aluminum: Some individuals worry if using aluminum cookware is dangerous. Based on research from the drug and food administration, National Institutes of Health, and the Alzheimer's Society of London, there are no health problems correlated with utilizing aluminum pans, pots, or skillets. "There is no conclusive diagnostic or scientific proof of a correlation between aluminum and Alzheimer's disease," says the Alzheimer's Society. While not a health concern, cooking cauliflower or leafy greens in aluminum cookware is not approved since it may influence the taste and appearance.

2. Non-stick coatings: Cookware fitted with a food-grade fluoropolymer can release poisonous fumes if severely overheated. Inhalation of these gases may trigger flu-like symptoms in humans, and pet birds are likely to be killed by them. Use care (for example, not to use it while broiling food) when cooking with non-stick cookware or consider using uncoated alternatives instead.

3. BPA: Bisphenol A (BPA) is a synthetic agent of considerable significance for older cookware. All cookware items that REI sells are BPA-free.

Other Cookware Considerations

1. Pot size: 1 pint per camper or backpacker in your group must be approximately the largest pot.

2. The amount of pots depends on the number of backpackers and the type of cooking you plan to do at your party. For two backpackers, if you are preparing to cook dehydrated stuff, one pot is enough. For more complicated meals and bigger teams, extra pans and pots are needed.

3. Lids: Lids minimize cooking time, conserve gasoline, and decrease splatter. Some cookware has a cover for each pot, while some have a single cover, which can be used on several pots of different sizes. Some lids may also serve as plates, which can lighten the load.

4. Pot grippers or lifters: Make sure you have a means of grabbing your pans and pots securely. Many cooking sets include one gripper for all of the pans. Remember to get it ready for you.

5. The benefits: Certain kitchen sets are filled with utensils, bowls, mugs, and even towels. This is helpful if you're beginning from zero or could be pointless if you're not.

Utensils

While traditional kitchen utensils can be used by car campers, many backpackers wanting to save weight and room have continued to gravitate to the Spork. This convenient mix of Spoons/forks provides tremendous flexibility. Few sporks often have a little knife on the side of an exterior tine.

Don't forget to bring measuring spoons, spatulas, and whisks, as needed.

Camp kitchen accessories

Campers should not have to "rough it" with these amenities onboard:

1. French press: This is a coffee maker (available for campers as well).

2. Extension forks: for roasting hot dogs or marshmallows.

3. Cooking Iron: for sandwiches which are to be grilled.

4. Dutch oven: For stews, meats, and more, a slow cooker.

5. Popcorn poppers: such a hit at a campfire.

6. Often, bring spice containers, squeeze bottles, and cleaning items.

3.3 How is a bonfire made?

For several, the campfire is a beloved and crucial outdoor tradition, a luminous, kinetic, dreamlike natural occurrence that for centuries has acted as the cornerstone of backwoods gatherings.

In this portion, the key steps for making a successful campfire are covered, and fire protection tips, whether you are camping in a car or backpacking.

1. Build a Fire Ring or Find

Campgrounds: Shape fires only in nominated fire circles, fireplaces, or grills. The majority of these constructed campsites have any variant. Using a fire ring will reveal the effects and hold fire contained.

Check with the campground operator periodically to make sure that fires are permitted. In certain places, intense dry cycles may trigger campfires to be banned, including in campgrounds.

Suppose you are camping with the land management department (U.S. Forest Service, Land Management Bureau, etc.) in an undeveloped area, search in-depth. It can include a permit for a campfire.

Assess the position before finally beginning the burn. Hold fire minimal or totally skip it whether the site has or is bushy with low-hanging trees. In dry conditions, fly-away flames could easily spark a wildfire.

Backcountry: Select an established fire ring in backcountry regions where wildfires are tolerated if one has been left behind. Create a new one only in emergency cases and, if the condition allows, dismantle it when you are done. If one still remains, scrub it out before you quit.

Clear out the fire pit with all the explosive stuff. Ideally, the base of the fires should be dirt, sand, or mineral soil (often seen on dirt bars or in streambeds). Intensive heat can sterilize good land, so pick your spot conscientiously.

An option to a fire pit is a mound-fire. Using a sanitation trowel, grow a round, smooth foundation of mineral soil (light-colored, sandy, no fertile dirt) around 6-8 inches thick. Use this as the foundation of your flames. Create this structure, ideally on a flat rock. You will easily disperse the mound until you are finished.

2. Firewood gathering

To burn a decent fire, you'll need three sources of fuel: kindling, tinder, and firewood.

Tinder uses tiny twigs, forest duff, dried leaves, or needles.

Kindling consists of tiny sticks, normally around less than an inch.

Firewood is some larger piece of wood that, for a long time, would hold fire going through the night.

Campgrounds: Please use nearby firewood. Nearby stores often carry firewood, and campground hosts also sell kindling or firewood kits for rent.

If you travel more than 50 miles to the south, don't bring wood with you. Campgrounds can also forbid the transport of your firewood, regardless of the distance you travel, to prevent the entry of troublesome insects into the area.

Contact the campground or a local ranger bureau in advance for updates and advice.

Backcountry: If you look for firewood, just pick up timber far from your place. Never kill dead or standing trees with live trees or broken branches. Wildlife and birds make use of snags and dead trees.

Must not collect or collect burned bits that are denser than the wrist of a grownup. This is because dense bits of wood are never required to be burnt completely & are typically left behind as unsightly, blackened fragments.

Notice that while harvesting timber, the rules of Leaving No Trace should be observed.

3. Create a Campfire for You

Cone: Start with a tiny burning cone around a few handfuls of Tinder, piled loosely in the middle of the ring of fire. If the fire is strong and the temperature increases, if required, you will add larger logs a couple at a time.

Log Cabin: Place two larger pieces of firewood parallel to each other and with some room in between to form your building frame. To build a square at the top and perpendicular, then turn 90 degrees and connect two slightly smaller bits. Place loads of tinder inside the square. Keep placing a couple more bits of firewood around the perimeter, getting a little smaller with each sheet. Finish with a layer of tinder and kindling above the end. Consider keeping room between logs to enable the fire to have enough

of oxygen available.

Upside down (pyramid): Starting side-by-side with three or four of your larger logs on the bottom sheet. Turn 90 degrees and then attach to the top of the comparatively smaller logs of the second layer. A couple more layers begin to alternate along this direction, getting thinner when you proceed. Place the Tinder on top of it, and your kindling.

4. The Campfire's Lighting

Enlighten the Tinder with a lighter or match. Using a fire starter that is designed to ignite fast, the Tinder will help catch the blaze. (Be sure to have the portable Firestarter and matches. Each of the Ten Necessities is required to include fire-making materials.)

After lighting the tinder, blast softly at the firebase to supply oxygen, which will significantly improve the power of the blaze and burn the wood more.

If the fire burns, move the embers to the center to consume them entirely. Preferably, you can restrict them to white ash,

5. Extinguish the campfire

Along with conventional land administrators, they also check their instructions and adopt their steps whether they have them. Generally, however, the fire can be extinguished by bucketing water on it (be cautious not to stay where you can be scald by the stream), rousing the ashes, and adding more water. Reprise as consistently as required. The Ashes must be cold to the touch until you leave the place. Be completely assured that the fire and its representatives are cold until you quit.

Remember that it is problematic to extinguish a fire with dust or sand so it can cover the coals, which can be exposed later, igniting a wildfire.

Warning! "Never leave a campfire unattended."

6. Cleaning up The Campfire

Burn garbage items only until they are fully eaten and transformed by fire to ash. Do not seek to use foil, cans, or plastic to ignite. When you burn everything that is not completely eaten, pick the remains when the fire is finished, and then pack it out or dump it in a waste container.

Pack away the trash that your pet contains when you're in the backcountry. Remove any residual charcoal pieces within your ring, remove them from your spot, shatter the chunks, and scatter the remains and dust over a wide region. Destroy whatever foundation you might have created.

3.4 How to set up and use a stove for gas?

Camping gas stoves may be used anywhere you need to prepare food, even without a refrigerator. Perhaps you could just be tailgating at a campground where fires are prohibited. Modern models of camping stoves have easy installation and are lightweight and portable. If you are out in the wilderness, it will benefit you to learn how to safely and easily use these stoves.

Setup of Stove

1. Remove all of the bits that came with the stove from the package. Generally speaking, camping stoves come in different separate sections that need to be linked. You get a pleasant summary of the things you have and work through taking all the bits from the backpack.

2. A sheet of paper or card with a description of the items to be used with the stove would be within the package. You will use this list to provide double-checking that you have it. A connecting pipe, gas tank, the stove should be there, and there may be a couple of other little items depending on what kind of stove you get.

3. If items are lacking, do not assemble the burner or stove since it can be dangerous.

4. Connect the gas canister to the stovetop by utilizing the gas cord. This is the primary relationship that needs to be established for you to be capable of cooking. The gas line will bind to the stove by twisting, but it may differ based on the kind of stove you have.

5. A metal jar is a canister, and usually, the gas line is made up of hose-like material.

6. Only be careful not to twist too hard. You will more likely detect a grinding sound if the gas line is already successfully connected.

7. Splash soapy water on gas connector sites in order to check for leakage. Wait until you have poured the water on them to observe whether any bubbles appear at the connection sites. If bubbles appear, this suggests a leaky link, and you can attempt to connect the gas line to the burner and canister again.

8. If there are no bubbles present, you are likely to continue.

9. The usage of some regular soap for dishwashing combined with water in a spray bottle fits well here.

10. If any leakage is coming from places that should not be there, the gas should also be set to 'off' here while you check.

11. Pat the contact points dry with a paper towel. If you leave these points moist, there is a risk of the remaining liquid preventing you from burning the burner.

12. When you do not have a paper towel, use a towel or some such mix of products.

13. Find a flat surface to place the burner on. When you are frying, the burner must be flat because there is a risk that it may fall over. This is not only dangerous, but it is potentially wasteful and extremely uncomfortable as well.

14. If you need to dig out some of the earth and stack it up to make a flat area, create a flat surface.

15. You should have the surface on which you have the stove as secure as practicable. Avoid some ground while you cook on it with the power to switch.

Operating the stove

1. Split the arms around the burner so they have spread apart evenly. The central help

where your pan would rest is these weapons. When the burner is crammed close, the weapons are crowded together. Spread them out by picking them and pushing them all over the burner.

2. Without these weapons extending into the right position, the stove will not have anything put on it since it would just be an open flame.

3. It is normal to have four arms, but there might be only three on your burner.

4. Using the canister's primer pump to pump the gas 15-20 cycles. This creates pressure build-up from the liquid fuel that is used to transform it from a form of liquid to a form of gas. Pump (about 15-20 pumps) until you can sense the heavy resistance of the pump.

5. The priming pump is usually a black pump at the top of the gas canister that can come out either vertically or horizontally.

6. This may require less or more pumps, and what the supplier of your specific stove advises must be looked at.

7. To take around 0.5 tsp (0.083 fl oz.) of fuel out, open the gas line. The petrol will go out to a limited catchment region where the blaze grows around it. This little bit of fuel is needed to heat the gas line to have a position where the liquid is turned into gas to burn effectively.

8. This would not need to be exactly 0.5 tsp (0.083 fl oz.). You need just a tiny amount of fuel in order to fire.

9. To open the gas line, turn the control knob that's attached to the burner. On the handle, it feels like a paperclip.

10. Flash the gasoline in the catchment area with a camp lighter or match. This procedure is called "priming" the gasoline, and it essentially plays the function of the spark on a regular stove by converting the liquid fuel in the pipe into a gas.

11. Using a long lighter or match to light up the fuel, and be careful not to burn your hand while you do this. When you touch the liquid with the flame, it will burn down really easily.

12. Let this fuel nearly fully burn out before going onto the next level.

13. Shift the fire to the scale that you need by using the adjuster. Now the stove is entirely

lit and able to be used as a consistent stove. Initializing the fuel adjuster then allows you a greater flame, and by turning it off, the flame is diminished.

14. The adjuster is normally connected to the burner, which appears like a paper clip that is hooked to the burner.

15. Be careful not to turn the fire down too much or to restart the stove; you will have to go through this planning phase again.

16. Get the configuration of your windbreak sheet. This is a thin layer constructed from aluminum that can be put around the stove to keep the breeze from disrupting the blaze. Many camping burners come with one, and they are a huge aid if you are cooking in windy conditions.

17. To work more effectively, set the windbreak sheet in a circle.

18. To hold it in position, bring any rocks along the side of the break if the wind is particularly strong.

19. Down cook. Now your stove's ready to cook. Using the fuel adjuster to alter how high the flame is. Before taking them away as they're sweaty, make sure that you let the pieces cool a little until you're finished.

20. Cooking on a small gas stove will take a little longer as the flame you are using is not nearly as hot as home burners, so be patient.

21. On these stoves, most styles of pans and pots operate great, but you can also roll food into a foil made of tin and cook it over the blaze.

3.5 With each occasion and season, what's the best food?

As long as the ingredients you have picked are light and flexible, it is one of the joys of camping to create a meal using just a couple of ingredients you have carried along. There are ten essential 'foundation' ingredients for making smart campsite dining dishes, whether you have a camping stove or have pre-made ingredients.

1. Halloumi

This firm sheep's milk cheese handles really well in a cold pocket as it maintains its form

and has a high melting point. The robust consistency of halloumi means that in blocks or slices, it can be baked to a very meat-like texture. Fry it or griddle it, then skewer it with some salad greens, then dressing to grill on a campfire or sell it in wraps.

2. Chickpeas

Ready-prepared canned chickpeas are much more versatile than the dry variety that needs soaking. Pour them straight into a bowl for a versatile side dish and dress them with vinegar, oil, and herbs. Add them to a jar or use them as the salad center, alternatively.

3. Flatbreads

Unlike an appropriate sandwich, flatbreads fold up into a tidy, portable collection, suitable for fitting into a hamper or rucksack. They can be turned into pizza, either eaten cold, smudged with hummus, or baked with traditional tomato toppings and cheese. Or, go and zip those melty quesadillas back, or use them to create a zingy chicken and lemon wrap.

4. Chorizo

Nestle it in your bag to find yourself a cured Spanish sausage of good size. Chorizo is the perfect camping sausage since it is ready-cured, so it can be consumed as a snack or diced, crisped up in an omelet to be enjoyed with smoky beans and eggs for breakfast as well, or combined with potatoes in a hash.

5. Sardines

All of the tinned fish is great for camping, but as sardines usually come in chunky fillets, they sound more like a whole meal. Serve sourdough bread for breakfast, zesty lemon and canned chickpeas for lunch, and fennel, spaghetti, and broccoli for dinner (not all on the same day.)

6. Eggs

They will have to be perched and held on top of your garments with relative caution, but eggs are ideal camping fodder. All kinds of fillings can be taken from omelets (it's a good way to use the chorizo). Eggy bread is a classic campsite breakfast as well.

7. Pooches of rice

The source for so many excellent meals, being among the most flexible grains, is rice.

And if they are already cooked, they are tiny and lightweight and can go from camping stoves to plastic plates in a couple of minutes. It can be applied as a burrito filling to a bean salad, converted into a hot and spicy curried pilaf, or made from Chinese-style egg fried rice.

8. Tinned fruits

When it comes to camp dessert, it's often a matter of combining rather than cooking. Tinned fruits may be combined into an immediate salad, so if you want to add a distinct touch, liquefy some caramel to sprinkle over tinned pears and scatter with hazelnuts. Sweet, shiny fresh cream peaches are also delicious.

9. Pasta

Pasta, regardless of form or scale, is a much-loved comfort ingredient that rules in a league of its own. Slender spaghetti is typically best for saving space, but once they have gone cold, fusilli and penne are more palatable. Create a carbonara with sausage as an alternative to bacon, bring together a new salad of pesto pasta, or melt the creamy cheese into a sauce of mushroom.

10. Ready-made dishes

Except in the oven, we're not worried about lasagna. One of the best ways for the campers to prepare is to make a one-pot dish that can be enjoyed off-site in homes. It is possible to serve pre-made meatballs or ragu and spillover spaghetti in tomato sauce, to eat the chili with campfire-baked potatoes, and to eat couscous with stew. Please only make sure everything has been adequately cooled and kept in a cold climate.

Chapter 4: Easy Camping Recipes

In this chapter, you will learn about the recipes to be used while on camping. All these recipes are carefully chosen that can be made by son to daughter and father to mother; in short, anyone can make these dishes. Another thing that is kept in mind while going for these recipes was one should take fewer things with them to avoid the burden of making these dishes. We hope once you go through these recipes, you'll know how easy to cook recipes are while on camping. So pack your bags, grab your stuff and enjoy these delicious dishes close to nature

4.1 Breakfast

1 Teriyaki Beef Jerky

Prep Time: 10 minutes, Cook Time: 4 hours, Serving 10, Difficulty: Difficult

(Nutrition) Per serving: Calories: 188kcal, Protein: 9g

Ingredients

- Sesame seeds (1 tsp.)

- Prague powder (¼ tsp.)

- Eye of round or top round (1 pound)

- Soy sauce (¼ cup)

- Mirin (2 tbsp.)

- Brown sugar (2 tbsp.)

- Prague powder (¼ tsp.)

- Piece of fresh ginger (1-inch), minced/pre-grated (1 tbsp.)

- Salt (1 tsp.)

- 2 cloves garlic, minced

Instructions

1. Round the beef into bits that are 1/8-1/4-inch-wide, eliminating as much noticeable fat as necessary. Put and set aside in a wide zip-top bag.

2. In a shallow cup, blend the brown sugar, soy sauce, mirin, minced ginger & garlic, cinnamon, and Prague powder until the sugar dissolves. Pour the meat into the zip-top container, taking care to ensure the meat is covered uniformly. Put the marinade in the fridge for 12-24 hours.

3. Place the strips on the dehydrator trays after the meat has cooked. Sprinkle the seeds with sesame. Dehydrate for 4-6 hours at 160F, before the meat has dried. If you bend a piece and it splits, the universal rule of thumb is that it's over-if you bend a piece and it falls; it's been fried too much longer.

4. Separate from the dehydrator and set it aside in a bag or Tupperware to cool fully prior to sealing.

5. Jerky marinated with Instacure or Prague powder can last at room temperature in a sealed bag for a few weeks. Jerky, marinated without any remedy, can stay in your fridge for two weeks.

2 Grab and Go Cranberry Granola Bars

Cook time: 30 mins, Total time: 30 mins, Serving 16, Difficulty: Normal

(Nutrition) Per serving: Calories: 148kcal, Protein: 19g

Ingredients:

- Salt (1/2 tsp.)

- Nonstick cooking spray

- Old-fashioned oats (2 c.)

- Water (2 tbsp.)

- Egg whites (2)

- Packed light brown sugar (2 tbsp.)

- Honey (1/2 c.)

- Ground cinnamon (1 tsp.)

- Wheat germ (3/4 c.)

- Vegetable Oil (1/2 c.)

- Chopped walnuts (3/4 c.)

- Dried cranberries (3/4 c.)

Instructions:

1. Preheat the oven to 325 ° F. s13- Spray with non - stick cooking spray on a 9-inch nonstick cooking tray. Pan with foil rows, leaving a 2-inch overhang, foil mist. Spread 2 cups of old-fashioned oats on a baking sheet: microwave fasts, at intervals of 1 min, 4-5 minutes, or until crispy and fragrant, stirring occasionally. Only let it cool. Whisk the honey, water, egg whites, light brown sugar, vegetable oil, ground cinnamon, and 1/2 tsp. salt in a big bowl until well mixed. Fold the oats and the toasted wheat germ, the sliced walnuts, and the dried cranberries; move them to the prepared pan. Press on even textures, utilizing wet hands.

2. Cook for 28 to 30 min or until the mixture is golden. Cool on a wire rack in a bowl. Switch to the cutting board using foil; slice into 16 bars. Store in an airtight jar for up to 4 days at room temperature or up to 1 month to freeze.

3 Peanut Butter & Jelly Granola Bars

Prep Time: 5 minutes, Cook Time: 28 minutes, Serving 6, Difficulty: Easy

Nutrition (Per Serving): Calories: 270kcal

Ingredients

- Peanuts (¼ cup chopped)

- Rolled oats (1 ½ cup)

- Salt (¼ tsp.)

- Jam (½ cup)

- Peanut butter (¼ cup)

- Coconut oil (1 tbsp.)

- Brown sugar (2 tbsp.)

Instructions

1. Preheat the oven to 350 with parchment paper or foil, cover a 9X5 loaf sheet.

2. Spread the oats for 10 minutes on a baking sheet and fry in the oven, adjusting at the 5-minute mark to confirm that they are uniformly toasted. Take it out of the oven and set it aside.

3. In a shallow saucepan, heat the jelly, peanut butter, sugar, oil, and salt. Simmer over medium heat for about 3 minutes until it thickens slightly, stirring continuously. Pour the toasted oats and swirl to thoroughly coat them in the pot.

4. Move the mixture in an even layer to the lined loaf dish. In the mixture, press the sliced peanuts onto the end.

5. Bake the bars until golden brown for 15 minutes. Take it out of the oven and leave to cool. Remove the rods from the pan and use a small knife to carve them into bars.

Notes

9x5 loaf pan Parchment paper or foil Baking sheet Small saucepan Mixing bowl Sharp

knife Measuring cups & spoons (Equipment needed)

4 Pear and Orange Muffins

Prep time: 20 mins, Total time: 55 mins, Serving 10, Difficulty: Normal

(Nutrition) Per serving: Calories: 192kcal, Protein: 12g

Ingredients

- Wheat bran (1 c.)

- Granulated sugar (1/2 c.)

- Olive oil (1/4 c.)

- Granulated sugar (2 tsp.)

- Medium red pear (1)

- Orange zest (2 tsp.)

- Egg (1)

- Whole-wheat flour (1 c.)

- Baking powder (1 tsp.)

- Buttermilk (1/2 c.)

- Baking soda (1/2 tsp.)

- Ground cinnamon (1/2 tsp.)

- Unsweetened applesauce (1/4 c.)

- Pinch Kosher salt (1)

Instructions:

1. Heat the oven to 350 degrees F and use ten paper liners to line a 12-hole muffin tray. Combine 2 tsp. of sugar and 2 tsp. of orange zest in a small cup. Set aside.

2. Mix the remaining 1/2 cup sugar, starch, baking powder, soda, cinnamon, wheat bran, and salt in a medium dish.

3. Put the applesauce, buttermilk, oil, and egg together in a large dish.

4. To the cup, add the flour mixture and blend to combine. In the batter, cut half the

pear into 1/4-inch bits and fold. Between the lined muffin cups, separate the batter.

5. Cut the remaining pear thinly and place it on the batter's level. Sprinkle with the orange sugar and bake for 25-30 min before a wooden pick inserted in the middle comes out clean.

6. For 5 minutes, let the muffins cool in the pan, then move to a wire rack.

5 Grilled Halloumi Breakfast Sandwich

Prep Time: 5 minutes, Cook Time: 15 minutes, Serving 1, Difficulty: Easy

Nutrition (Per Serving): Calories: 651kcal

Equipment

- Camp Stove

Ingredients

- Salt + pepper (to taste)

- 1 large Hawaiian sweet roll (use the sandwich buns if you can find them)

- 1 scallion (sliced or julienned)

- Butter/oil (1 tbsp.- divided)

- Sriracha (1 tbsp.-more/less depending on your heat preference)

- Halloumi cheese (2 oz.- sliced)

- Mayo (3 tbsp.)

- 1 egg

Instructions

1. Or in your pan or over a fire, toast the sandwich buns. Only put aside.

2. Over medium-high melt, melt half the butter or oil in your skillet. Add the cheese until melted. Fry in spots on either side until golden brown, between 3-4 minutes on each side. Only put aside. If you've got one going, this move may also be achieved on a barbecue.

Miss the butter/oil in that case and put the cheese directly on the grill.

3. Over a medium melt, heat the remaining butter or oil. Crack the egg into the pan until it is melted. Totally optional step: You can use a fork to blend the yolk a little until the whites begin to set so that it gets spread a little across the egg, so in every bite, there will be yolk. Cook the egg for about 4 minutes or until it's cooked to the perfect amount of doneness.

4. Prep the hot mayo when the egg is boiling. Mix the mayo and the Sriracha together in a small bowl (or in a measuring cup).

5. To assemble, on each cut surface of the buns, spread the spicy mayo in Layer to sample with the egg, scallions, grilled halloumi, and salt & pepper.

6 Camping Breakfast Burritos

Prep time: 15 minutes, Cook time: 30 minutes, Total time: 45 minutes, Serving 8, Difficulty: Normal

(Nutrition) Per serving: Calories: 188kcal, Protein: 9g

Ingredients:

- Olive oil (1/2 tbsp.)

- Frozen hash browns (1 cup)

- Cooked ham (8 oz.-diced)

- Eggs (12)

- Old El Paso Taco Seasoning (1 tbsp.)

- 12-inch Old El Paso flour tortillas (8)

- Old El Paso Green Chiles (1) (4.5 oz.)

- Chopped cilantro (1/4 cup)

- Shredded cheddar cheese (2 cups-8 oz.)

Instructions:

1. In a large skillet, heat the olive oil. Add the hash browns and cook, stirring continuously, for 1 minute. In the ham, add. Continue cooking, stirring regularly, until both the hash

browns and the ham have browned, around 8-10 minutes.

2. Meanwhile, whisk the eggs gently in a large bowl. In the taco seasoning, whisk. When browned with the hash browns and ham, pour the eggs into the pan. Cook, constantly stirring, until the eggs are ready. Stir in the cilantro, cheese, and green chilies.

3. Tortillas warm up. Lower the middle of each tortilla with 1/8 of the egg mixture. Roll up and roll securely in foil like a burrito. Hold it in a refrigerator or cooler in a zip-top pocket.

4. Put wrapped burritos in hot coals by the fire until ready to cook. Let the burritos remain in the coal, rotating once, around 10-15 minutes until heated through. (How hot your fire is will depend on the time.)

7 Sweet & Spicy Breakfast Skillet

Prep Time: 5 minutes, Cook Time: 20 min, Serving 2, Difficulty: Easy

Nutrition (Per Serving): Calories: 251kcal

Ingredients

- Olive oil (1 tbsp.)

- Sweet potato (1 large- cut into 1/2-inch cubes)

- Poblano peppers (2) stems removed-cut into 1/2-inch pieces

- Salt (1/2 tsp.)

- Kale (2 cups-chopped)

- Cloves garlic (3-minced)

- Eggs (2)

Instructions

1. Heat olive oil over med-high heat in a skillet. Stir in the tomatoes, sweet potato, and half tsp. salt until the oil starts to shimmer. Cook for 7 to 10 minutes before softening

starts, stirring regularly so that the vegetables are cooked uniformly. Add the kale and garlic and simmer until the kale is soft for an additional 3-5 minutes.

2. Shift them over to one side of the skillet until the vegetables are finished.

3. If needed, add further oil, then into the empty half of the skillet, beat the eggs. Cook until you like the eggs; we want them fried in the center but always runny.

4. Season with pepper and salt, break between two bowls and enjoy.

8 Mountain Man Breakfast Casserole

Cook Time: 40 min, Serving 8, Difficulty: Normal

(Nutrition) Per serving: Calories: 188kcal, Protein: 9g

Ingredients:

- Salt and pepper (to taste)

- Pound pork sausage (1)

- Eggs (1 dozen-whisked)

- Cheddar cheese-diced (1 cup)

- Simply Potatoes (2 packages- hash browns or diced)

- Large onion (1-chopped)

Instructions:

1. Brown the sausage over a heavy coal fire in a cast-iron. On paper towels, cut and rinse the sausage.

1. Sauté the onion until soft in the remaining drippings. Remove the potatoes and mix them until they are finely browned and crispy. Spread the potatoes with the ham, eggs, and cheese equally on the bottom and back. Place the lid top and apply the roof to 16 hot coals.

2. Bake until the eggs are ready, for 25 minutes. Just serve.

9 Breakfast Scramble with Sun-Dried Peppers and Spinach

Prep Time: 5 minutes, Cook Time: 10 minutes, Serving 2, Difficulty: Easy

Nutrition (Per Serving): Calories: 313kcal

Ingredients

- Ova Easy (cup 3/4)

- Water (1 ¼ cup-10 oz.)

- Sun-dried peppers (1/2 cup chopped)

- 1 tbsp. olive oil/1 packet olive oil

- Dehydrated spinach (cup 1/2)

- Garlic powder (1/2 tsp.)

- Ground black pepper (1/2 tsp.)

- Salt (1/2 tsp.)

Instructions

1. **At home:** In a zip lock or little jar, apply the Ova Easy and spices (pepper, garlic powder, and salt), spinach, and peppers (large enough to add water at camp and blend).

2. **At camp:** To the baggie of eggs & vegetables, add 1 1/4 cup (10 oz.) water. When fully mixed, blend with a fork or spoon, and no lumps of egg left. Put aside so that the spinach has time, about three minutes, to rehydrate.

3. Heat the oil in a boiling pot or pan over low heat. .Add the peppers and spinach, and egg mixture. Using a spoon, mix the eggs as they cook, taking care not to scorch the eggs until in the pot there is no liquid egg left if the pan is small. Yeah. Dig deep.

10 Campfire Breakfast Burger Recipe

Prep time: 25 minutes, Cook time: 25 minutes, Total time: 40 minutes, Serving 12, Difficulty: Normal

(Nutrition) Per serving: Calories: 238kcal, Protein: 13g

Ingredients:

- Sugar (1 tbsp.)

- Flour (2 cups)

- Salt (1 tsp.)

- Baking powder (3 tsp.)

- Eggs (12)

- Dry milk powder (6 tbsp.)

- Sausage patties (12)

- Black pepper (2 tsp.)

- Canola oil (4 tbsp.)

- Water (1 cup)

- Shredded cheddar cheese (1/2 cup)

Instructions:

1. Mix flour, baking powder, sugar, cinnamon, dried milk powder, canola oil, and black pepper in a medium bowl until well mixed. Pour the dried mixture into a medium-sized bowl and squeeze 1/2 cup of water to blend the biscuits. Slowly apply 1 tbsp. At a time to the remaining half cup of water until the biscuit mix is thick. Stir in the cheese with the cheddar. Over medium fire, set the cast iron pan and apply oil to the coating. Scoop biscuit mix into the plate with the meager 1/4 cup (you will need to function in tiny batches). Enable it to cook until golden brown on the first side and flip once. Cook until the biscuits are baked and moist.

2. In a cold cast iron pan, introduce the sausage and place it over medium-high heat. Cook until the sausages are golden brown, turning once, then cooked thru. Withdraw and put aside.

3. Cook eggs up to the perfect doneness in a cast-iron skillet (I prefer my yolks a little runny). Break the biscuits in two and cover them with the egg and bacon. If needed, add ketchup or hot sauce and put another half of the biscuit on top.

4.2 Lunch Recipes

1 Campfire Skillet Cornbread

Prep Time: 5 min Cook Time: 20 min Serving: 8, Difficulty: Easy

Per serving kcal: 127

Ingredients:

- Oil ½ tbsp.

- Med grind cornmeal 1 cup

- Honey 2 tbsp.

- Flour 1/2 cup

- Baking powder 1 tbsp.

- Egg 1

- Salt 1/2 tsp.

- Milk 1 cup

Instructions:

1. Combine the flour, cornmeal, salt & baking powder in a wide bowl.

2. In dry ingredients, add the egg, honey & milk. Mix it till completely combined.

3. Heat oil in the cast-iron pan above the campfire. And coat its bottom, swirl. Place the batter in the pan, making sure all is in the even layer. Cover the pan with foil crimping a foil across the corners.

4. Cook for fifteen min on med-low heat, then step away from the heat & allow the bread to rest for an extra five min (also now covered). Cut it into slices & enjoy it.

Note

You can make basic cast iron skillet cornbread fast on the right over the campfire.

2 Campfire Grilled Chicken Panini

Prep time: 5 minutes, Cook time: 20 minutes, Total time: 25 minutes, Serving 4, Difficulty: Easy

Per serving kcal: 159

Ingredients:

- Ciabatta rolls (4)

- Boneless, skinless chicken breast chopped (1 1bs)

- Cheddar cheese (2-4 oz. sliced thin)

- Salt and pepper (to taste)

- Mayo (2 tbsp.)

- Oil (for grill grate)

- Butter (1 tbsp.)

- Granny smith apple (1-sliced)

- Onion sliced (1/4 – sliced)

- Red pepper (1/2- seeded and sliced)

Instructions:

1. For indirect cooking, heat your grill and clean and oil the grater.

2. "Pat the chicken dry when ready to cook (I used charcoal), then pound to 1/2" thick.

3. This can be done in preparation and frozen in ziplock bags before ready to cook before coming in; make sure that the chicken is placed on ice at a safe temperature.

4. Season the salt and pepper with the chicken and toss it on the grill.

5. Cover and cook until the chicken reads 160 degrees on an instant thermometer, turning as needed for epic grill marks (and to make sure the heat is uniformly distributed).

6. Cover and let rest another 5 degrees in foil.

7. Meanwhile, toss in the oil with the sliced peppers and onion, sprinkle with a little spice, throw in a safe campfire pan or griddle, and cook until soft.

8. Slide the chicken and add the onion and pepper to toss.

9. Slather in mayo the wraps, place over the wraps the sliced apples, poultry, onions, peppers, and cheese, and finish with the other half of the sheet.

10. Cover and push into the campfire firmly in foil until the bread is cooked through and the cheese is melty.

11. If you have a safe way to grab your sandwiches, no need to make sacrifices to the camping gods; this can be done by tossing the foil directly into the campfire. By pressing the wrapped sandwiches with the newly used griddle for delicious grill marks, make a Panini.

12. Unwrap, serve hot.

3 Sweet & Savory Grilled Tempeh

Prep Time: 30 min Cook Time: 5 min Serving: 4, Difficulty: Normal

Per serving kcal: 167

Ingredients:

- Maple syrup 1/4 cup

- Apple cider vinegar 1 tbsp.

- Soy sauce 2 tbsp.

- Tempeh 8 oz.

Instructions:

1. In a zip-lock plastic bag wide enough to carry the tempeh, mix the soya sauce, apple cider vinegar & maple syrup.

2. Slice your tempeh into four slices. With marinade, put them within a zip lock bag. Be sure that the slices of tempeh are equally coated & allow for at least thirty min to marinate.

3. Grill/barbecue the tempeh on the campfire or roast it with a hint of oil in the cast iron pan. Cook on both sides for 2 to 3 mins.

4 Grilled Sesame Shrimp & Veggies

Prep time: 10 minutes, Cook time: 10 minutes, Total time: 20 minutes, Serving 6, Difficulty: Easy

Per serving kcal: 210

Ingredients:

- Mushrooms (2 cups-sliced)
- Shrimp (1 cup- uncooked, tail off, deveined and peeled)
- Large onion (1-sliced)
- Sugar snap peas (2/3 cup)
- Green peppers (2-sliced)
- Yellow peppers (2-sliced)
- Red peppers (2- sliced)

Sauce:

- Cloves garlic (4- minced)
- Blue Dragon Sesame Oil (1/2 cup)
- Sesame seeds (2 tsp.)
- Rice vinegar (6 tbsp.)

Instructions:

1. In a bowl, toss the vegetables together.

2. Six sheets of aluminum foil, around the size of a 9-13 baking sheet, are cut and placed on a flat surface.

3. To each sheet, add around 1 1/2 cups of veggies on one side. Divide the shrimp uniformly and put it on top of the veggies.

4. Whisk together the ingredients for the sauce in a small bowl. To each shrimp & veggie mixture, apply around 2 tbsp. of sauce and move about slowly using a spoon to combine.

5. To make a packet, roll up the aluminum foil. To seal, fold the ends.

6. On medium-high heat, grill for 10 minutes. Serve it hot.

5 Shakshuka

Prep Time: 5 min Cook Time: 20 min Serving: 2, Difficulty: Easy

Per serving Net carbs: 23g fiber: 5g Fat: 16g Protein: 12g kcal: 276

Ingredients:

- Pepper & Salt

- Olive oil 1 tbsp.

- Minced parsley

- Seeded & sliced red bell pepper 1

- Feta cheese 1/4 cup

- Sliced & seeded poblano peppers 1

- Diced small onion 1

- Diced tomatoes 14 oz. can

- Chopped garlic 3 cloves

- Cumin 1 tsp.

- Paprika 2 tsp.

Instructions:

1. Warm oil over low heat in your pan. When the poblano, red bell peppers & onions are warmed, swirl to cover, & cook for five mins or until its color changes to brown, stirring if required. Put the paprika, cumin & garlic, then cook for around thirty sec till it is fragrant.

2. Place the tomatoes as well as their juices. To allow the combination to thicken, lower the heat & boil for ten min.

3. Break the eggs into the sauce, uniformly spaced them apart. Cover & let the eggs boil till the whites are set, 5 to 7 mins. To allow them to cook completely, you may spoon that sauce over the top as required.

4. Top to taste. Serve with feta cheese, sliced parsley, and a couple of pieces of crusty bread.

6 Campfire bread on a stick

Prep time: 10 minutes, Cook time: 10 minutes, Total Time: 20 minutes, Serving 8, Difficulty: Easy

Per serving kcal: 148

Ingredients:

- Salt (1 tsp.)

- Dried yeast (1 tsp.)

- Olive oil (2 tbsp.)(30 ml)

- Sugar (1 tsp.)

- Warm water (7/8 cup)(200 ml)

- Flour (2 1/2 cups)(300 g)

Instructions:

Dough

1. Mix all the ingredients into a moist dough in a large bowl. No kneading required.

2. Cover the bowl and let the dough rise until it has doubled in size, around 1 hour in a warm place.

3. 'Knockback' the dough briefly with floured hands by making it into a ball.

4. Tip the dough out and divide it into eight parts on a floured surface.

Shaping your stick bread

1. Begin by stretching a strip of the dough and then rolling it into a long sausage shape.

2. Twist a strip around the sticks at the end. If need be, pinch the dough together to secure the top.

Cooking over a campfire:

1. Just keep your stick over the fire or prop it up.

2. For better results, choose a spot over hot embers.

3. Keep rotating until you have browned both parts.

4. Enjoy your bread that was freshly baked.

7 Dutch Oven Chicken Marbella

Prep Time: 5 min Cook Time: 45 min Serving: 4, Difficulty: Normal

Per serving kcal: 475

Ingredients:

- Olive oil 1 tbsp.
- Chopped prunes 1 cup
- Skin-on chicken thighs 4
- Halved & pitted olives 1 cup
- Dry white wine 1/2 cup
- Salt 1 tsp.

- Capers 1/4 cup

- Red wine vinegar 1/4 cup

- Bay leaves 2

- Roughly minced garlic 6 cloves

- Dried oregano 2 tbsp.

- Brown Sugar 4 tsp.

Instructions:

1. Marinate the chicken: put the bag in the freezer to marinate all ingredients except the brown sugar & oil. For at least six hrs. & up to 2 days, put in your icebox.

2. Prepare the campfire: twenty-seven prep coals. If you need to, you could use wood embers, although you'll have to measure the right heat ratio (you're looking for 220 c).when all the coals are fully prepared, knock them into just a plain pile & put them all on top of the Dutch oven. This would produce the higher heat needed for browning.

3. Brown the chicken: in the Dutch oven, heat 1 tbsp. of oil. The oil is ready & hot once the water drops sizzles as it hits the skillet. Take your chicken from marinade, then brush 1 tsp. of brown sugar over both thigh's skin side. Brown the thighs' skin side at high temperature till the skin becomes crispy & its color changes to a deep golden brown, around 6-8 mins. Please turn to the other side for two mins to brown it.

4. Bake: turn off the Dutch oven heat. Put the marinade in the oven of Dutch & cover. Spread 18 coals equally on the lid and put nine coals in the oven of Dutch. Bake for thirty mins till the thighs are fully cooked & with there, juices run clear once stabbed with a knife.

5. Serve and enjoy with a few of a sauce spooned on the top, serve it over couscous, pilaf/rice.

8 Grilled Potatoes:

Prep time: 10 mins, Cook time: 20 mins, Total time: 30 mins, Serving 4, Difficulty: Easy

Per serving kcal: 143

Ingredients:

- Red potatoes (2 1ls.)
- Pepper (1/8 tsp.)
- Olive oil (1/4 cup)
- Salt (1 tsp.)
- Potato Seasoning
- Rosemary (1 tsp.)
- Oregano (3/4 tsp.)
- Nutmeg (1/8 tsp.)
- Thyme (3/4 tsp.)
- Sage (3/4 tsp.)

Instructions:

1. For the seasoning of potato, mix the spices. To mix, pour the olive oil (much of it) over the spice mix, then stir well. When required, add the left oil to the potatoes.

2. Into strips that are 1/2-inch-thick, slice the potatoes. Prefer to slice the circular ends thinly so that the potato on each side will lay on the grill flat.

3. In a large bowl, put the potato slices and drizzle with the seasoning/olive oil mix. Toss well to mix.

4. Preheat to med-high heat on the grill.

5. Two large sheets of foil are layered down & lightly sprayed with the cooking spray.

6. Put the potatoes in a layer, if necessary, on top of the foil. Cover it with foil & seal it shut.

7. On the grill, put the foil packet and close the lid. 20-minute heat.

8. For flipping the potatoes, use kitchen tongs and heat, uncovered, for a further 5-10 mins.

9. Remove and enjoy

9 Sweet + Spicy Cashew Chicken Wrap

Prep time 3 min, Total time 3 minutes, Serving 2, Difficulty: Easy

(Nutrition) Per serving: Calories: 450kcal, Protein: 28g

Ingredients

- Cooked chicken (1 7oz packet)
- Dried cilantro (1 tsp.)
- Cashews (½ cup-chopped)
- Tortillas/wraps (2)
- Sriracha (packets 1-2)
- Honey (2 packets-2 tbsp.)
- Mayo (2 packets-2 tbsp.)
- Salt

Instructions

1. Place the cashews, sugar, mayo, Sriracha packs, coriander, and salt in a bag at home. Load the bag along with the cashews and the chicken pocket.

2. Drain the chicken if required at the camp. Add the chicken with the cashews, butter, Sriracha, cilantro, mayo, and salt and stir to mix. Spoon the mixture of chicken onto the tortillas. Roll up burrito-style for them and enjoy.

10 Chicken & Potato Foil Packets

Prep time: 15 mins, Cook time: 30 mins, Total time: 45 mins, Serving 4, Difficulty: Normal

Per serving kcal: 167

Ingredients:

- Sour cream (4 tbsp.)

- Thinly sliced Baby potatoes (1 1/2 lbs.)

- Green onions/Chives

- Olive oil (2 tsp.)

- Divided Barbecue sauce (1 cup)

- Seasoning salt (1 tbsp.)

- Pepper (1/4 tsp.)

- Boneless skinless chicken breasts (4)

- Shredded Cheddar cheese (2/3 cup)

- Bacon bits (1/4 cup)

Instructions:

1. Preheat the grill to med-high heat.

2. Prepare packets of foil. Spread out four big heavy-duty foil pieces, then top each one with a parchment paper big piece (or spray with a nonstick spray).

3. In the center of each packet, placed equivalent numbers of sliced onions and potatoes. Add oil and sprinkle with pepper and salt to season.

4. Place the chicken breast on the potatoes top. Using barbecue sauce to brush all sides of every chicken breast.

5. By bringing two sides together and folding them out, tie up every foil packet. Then, to close the package, roll up all open ends.

6. Place on a hot grill and cook for around 25 mins (potatoes down) or till tender & chicken is cooked (chicken must be 165 ° F).

7. Top with bacon pieces and cheddar cheese, break open package, brush chicken with even more barbecue sauce. Put it on the grill again to melt for around 5 mins (don't reseal).

8. Garnish with chives and sour cream.

Notes:

Depending on the size of the chicken breasts as well as the potato's thickness, cooking time varies. Make sure the chicken reaches 165 ° F and soften the potatoes.

4.3 Dinner Recipes

1 Drunken Cauliflower Tacos with Quick Pickled Red Onions

Prep Time: 5 min Cook Time: 20 min Serving: 6 Difficulty: Easy

Per serving kcal: 107

Ingredients:

Cauliflower Tacos

- Corn tortillas 6

- Chopped cauliflower 1 head

- Minced garlic 2 cloves

- Lager 1/2 cup

- Cumin 2 tbsp.

- Olive oil 1 tbsp.

- Dried oregano 2 tsp.

- Cayenne 1/8 tsp.

- Sea salt 1 tsp.

Quick pickled onions

- Sliced red onion 1 small

- Juiced limes 2/3

Instructions:

1. Prepare the fast-pickled onions: in a tiny bowl, add the lime juice, salt & onions. Have them stay for around 15 to 20 min, tossing per five min

2. Cook the cauliflower: put cumin, beer, salt, dried oregano, garlic & cayenne to the cauliflower in a pan. Carry to a boil fast. Boil till all of the liquid has vaporized, stirring regularly. If the liquid has vaporized, put the olive oil and fry till the cauliflower is soft and brown at the beginning.

3. Heat the tortillas: Heat the tortillas when the cauliflower is frying. We do this for 1 tortilla at the moment in the stove burner, rotating every 15-20 sec so that all sides are toasty. This may be completed on a campfire as well, or in the oven, if you're at home.

4. Assemble the tacos: fill every tortilla with the scoop of pickled red onions, cauliflower, and some extra toppings

2 Teriyaki Shrimp Foil Packets

Cook time: 10 mins, Prep time: 10 mins, Total time: 20 mins, Serving 4, Difficulty: Easy

Per serving kcal: 153

Ingredients:

- Rice/cold cooked (2 cups)

- Pineapple chunks (20 ounces- 1 cup drain)

- Green pepper Large (1-cut in 1 & ½ "pieces)

- Red bell peppers Large (2 - cut in 1 & ½ "pieces)

- Snap peas (3 cups)

- Teriyaki sauce (1 & ½ cups-divided)

- Clove minced garlic (1)

- Shrimp 1 lb. (peeled & deveined)

- Freshly grated ginger (2 tsp.)

- For garnish Green onions & sesame seeds

- Olive oil (2 tbsp.)

Instructions:

1. Preheat the grill to 425 ° F (med-high heat). Prepare 4 sheets of heavy-duty foil (12 x 18 ") and spray it with cooking spray.

2. Combine the pineapple, green and red peppers, snap peas, ginger, garlic, and one cup of teriyaki sauce in some big bowl. To coat uniformly, toss.

3. Divide the rice, vegetable mixture & shrimp equally (in order) on every foil sheet.

4. With olive oil, drizzle it, season with pepper and salt, and then drizzle with 1/2 cup of teriyaki sauce leftover.

5. Seal every foil packet well and shrimp side down on the hot grill.

6. Cook 5 mins, turn over, and for an extra 4 mins, cook rice side down.

7. Remove from the grill and let it rest before serving for 2-3 mins. Fold the foil back gently and garnish with the sesame seeds and green onions.

8. If needed, drizzle with extra teriyaki sauce.

3 Artichoke & Poblano Campfire Paella

Prep Time: 5 min Cook Time: 40 min Serving: 2, Difficulty: Normal

Per serving 30g kcal: 300

Ingredients:

- Saffron pinch

- Olive 2 tbsp.

- Poblano peppers 2

- Diced shallot 1 large

- Green onions 3

- Halved & drained artichoke hearts 14 oz. can

- Rice 1/2 cup

- Roughly minced garlic 3 cloves

- Broth 14 oz. can

- Tempranillo 1/4 cup

- Salt 1/2 tsp.

Instructions:

1. Put the green onions, sausage & poblanos peppers directly on the fire on the grill pan, rotating periodically, till the onions & peppers are tender & crispy & the sausage is cooked completely. Take it from your grill. Cut your sausage into pieces of around 1/4 inch. Let the peppers to chill, extract the seeds, peel the skin off, & chop. Mince the green onions into bite-sized bits.

2. Put the cast iron pan straight on over fire on the barbecue/grill. To cover the bottom of the pan, add plenty of oil & then place the shallots. Sauté for 3 to 5 mins till it is smooth. Place the garlic & sliced sausage & sauté for around 30 sec, till the garlic is aromatic. Put the rice & cook for 2 to 3 mins, often mixing till the ends are only translucent. Place 1/4 cup red wine in the skillet, allow to vaporize. After that, put the broth. Add salt as well as a pinch of saffron to season. Mix well to spread all the ingredients equally, and then leave 20 to 30 mins to boil, undisturbed, till all the liquid has been absorbed.

3. To reheat, add to the skillet the sliced green onions, artichoke hearts & poblanos. At that moment, the paella on the bottom will start forming the Socarrat. You would start hearing the rice beginning to crackle within a few mins. That's the sign here that the dish is almost finished. To ensure that the Socarrat has formed, cook for another few mins.

4. Serve quickly.

Note

With tasty veggies & spices, this pan campfire paella could be made vegan/gluten-free.

4 Camping Hotdog Recipe for the Campfire

Prep Time: 5 min Cook Time: 20 min Serving: 2, Difficulty: Easy

Per serving kcal: 160

Ingredients:

- Pillsbury crescent rolls

- Hot dogs

Instructions:

1. Place a skewer about ¾."

2. Open the crescent rolls and wrap around each hot dog, beginning with the flat end of the crescent and finishing with the tip of the triangle, one long pre-cut triangle.

3. Using aluminum foil to wrap the crescent covered hot dogs loosely.

4. Roast over the fire, much as you might roast a hot dog when turning your stick.

5. For 15-20 minutes, cook.

6. Serve with ketchup and mustard.

Instructions: (For Hotdogs over a campfire)

1. Place a skewer * approximately ¾" at the end of your hot dogs.

2. Open the crescent rolls and wrap around each hot dog, started with the flat end of the crescent and finishing with the tip of the triangle, one long pre-cut triangle.

3. Using aluminum foil to wrap the crescent covered hot dogs loosely.

4. Roast over the fire, much as you might roast a hot dog when turning your stick.

5. Cook the hot dogs for 15-20 minutes over a campfire.

6. Uncover the foil.

7. Using a side of ketchup and mustard to serve.

8. Enjoy

5 Campfire Pizza Margherita

Prep Time: 25 min Cook Time: 15 min Serving: 2, Difficulty: Normal

Per serving kcal: 1150

Ingredients:

For the crust

- Olive oil 5 tbsp.

- Flour 2 ½ cups

- Warm water 1 cup

- Rapid rise yeast 1 packet

- Salt 2 tsp.

Toppings

- Tomato sauce 1/2 cup

- Cut into 1/4-inch rounds mozzarella ball 8 oz.

- Cut into ribbons fresh basil 2 tbsp.

- Sliced into 1/4-inch tomato 1 large

Instructions:

1. Add the yeast, salt & flour into a food processor or bowl. To split the ingredients, gently combine with a fork.

2. To dry ingredients, add the hot water and 2 tbsp. of oil & combine with the fork till the ingredients start to shape the dough.

3. Knead your dough a couple of times, so all the components are very well combined & the dough stays together.

4. Cover your dough for twenty mins & allow it to rise.

5. Turn it out on a chopping board once your dough has risen, then split the dough into two separate parts.

6. In a 10-inch cast-iron pan, put 1 tbsp. oil to make the crust & swirl to cover the top. Put one of the dough halves within the pan, push & press the dough into the pan's sides with the fingers. Sprinkle 1/2 tbsp. of oil with the sides of the pan.

7. Put the pan at suitably high heat on a grate on the campfire/camp stove. Cook for 3 to 5 mins, till the bottom, has tightened up & starts to change to a golden brown.

8. Remove the pan from the heat & put it on a heat-safe surface. The pan would be hot, so stay aware of the next few stages.

9. Take a crust out from the pan by using two tongs & flip it so that the pan's non-cooked part is face-down.

10. Split tomato sauce 1/4 cup over on the top of the pizza; after this, layer the minced tomatoes & mozzarella. Season the top with basil.

11. Bring the pizza to the stove/campfire. Cook the pizza till the bottom becomes golden brown for 3 to 5 mins. After some mins, remove the foil or lid when the cheese is melted to allow the steam to escape for the rest of the cooking period,

12. Remove the pan from the oven, move the pizza safely to a dish & repeat for the second half of the dough.

6 Walking Taco Easy Campfire Recipe

Prep time: 20 mins, Cook time: 30 mins, Total time: 50 mins, Difficulty: Normal

Per serving kcal: 125

Ingredients:

- Cheese of Monterey Jack (1 cup shredded)

- Bacon grease (1 tbsp.)

- Ground beef (1 pound)

- Med yellow onion (1/2 - chopped)

- Nacho Cheese Doritos (5 1-ounce bags)

- Salsa (3/4 cup)

- Lettuce (1 cup-chopped/shredded)

- Sour cream (3/4 cup)

- Avocados (2-peeled & chopped)

- Cheddar cheese (1 cup shredded)

- Tomatoes (1 cup- diced)

Instructions:

1. You may choose to cook on the camp stove, on a grill, or on a campfire. When possible, cook over a fire.

2. At this stage, the fire must be down to the coals, with a little bit of fire here and there. Right over the coals, we tend to use our tripod barbecue. The grill's height over a fire will need to be adjusted, so the pan does not get very hot that the meat burns.

3. Sauté the onion (chopped) in bacon grease melted /olive oil in a large cast-iron skillet.

4. Then, put the ground beef then combine it with onion, sometimes stirring when cooking the mixture.

5. Meanwhile, chop up the cabbage, tomatoes, and avocados while waiting for the meat cooking.

6. When cooked is the meat, go further and drain it safely.

7. Then stir the meat with the salsa.

8. Allow a further 5-10 mins for the mixture to cook.

9. Open the chip bags and smash the chips a bit if you like.

10. Add the beef mixture (ground).

11. Then add your favorite toppings and a sour cream dollop. We add tomatoes, lettuce, and avocados.

12. Sprinkle with the cheese that has been shredded.

13. Using a fork, giving it all a quick swirl, mix it all up well.

14. And it's good to eat then

7 Moroccan Chicken Couscous

Prep Time: 5 min Cook Time: 5 min Serving: 2, Difficulty: Easy

Per serving Net carbs: 79g fiber: 12g Fat: 24g Protein: 40g kcal: 665

Equipment

- Backpacking stove

- Backpacking pot

Ingredients:

- Chopped dried apricots 1 cup

- Couscous ½ cup

- Sea salt 1 tsp.

- Sliced almonds ¼ cup

- Olive oil 2 tbsp.

- Raps el Hanout 4 tsp.

- Cooked chicken 7 oz. packet

- Water 5 oz.

- True lemon 1 packet

Instructions:

1. At home: in a resalable plastic bag, put the apricots, couscous, almonds, salt & raps el Hanout. Pack the packets of the chicken pouch, true lemon & olive oil.

2. At camp: in the cookpot, put ~5 oz. of water & oil to a boil. Then put to the pot the apricots, couscous, spices, true lemon & nuts. To mix, give it a major shake, put it to the chicken, then cover & take it from the heat. Let sit for five mins.

Note

Make it vegan/vegetarian

By swapping the chicken with a protein source like the TVP/soy curls, this could easily be turned vegetarian/vegan.

8 Campfire Stew

Prep Time: 10 mins, Cook time: 50 mins, Total time: 1 hour, Serving 6, Difficulty: Difficult

Calories: 358kcal

Ingredients:

- Pork shoulder without bone (1.4 kg)

- Olive oil (1 tbsp.)

- Peppers bell (2- deseeded & finely chopped)

- Onion (1- chopped finely)

- Beans Black-eyed (2 tin-drained)

- Garlic cloves (2- minced)

- Dried mixed herbs (2 tsp.)

- Chopped tomatoes (1 cup)

- Smoked paprika (2 tsp.)

- Tomato puree (2 tbsp.)

- Water or stock (100 ml)

- Caraway seeds (2 tsp.)

- Salt

- Black pepper

Instructions:

Campfire

1. Increase the sum to 1 liter of water/stock and dice the meat in pieces of bite-size.

2. In a big pot, heat the oil and sauté onions until soft for 5 min. (optional step)

3. Then put the meat for 5 min and brown. (Optional step)

4. Add the garlic until fragrant for 1 minute and then add in the ingredients.

5. Put to a boil, lower to a simmer, cook after covering the pot till the meat is soft for 1-5-2hrs. Keep an eye out for water since you might require adding a bit more.

6. Adjust and serve with seasoning.

7. If you don't want liquid (extra) at the cooking end, then simmer uncovered stew for 10 to 15 minutes for thickening it. (Optional step)

9 Pie Iron Pizza Pockets

Prep time 30 min, Cook time 15 min, Serving 4 pizza pockets, Difficulty: Normal

Per serving: Net carbs: 63 g, Fat: 23 g, Protein: 18 g, kcal: 550

Ingredients

Pizza Dough

- Rapid rise yeast 1 packet

- All-purpose Flour 2 ¾ cups

- Olive Oil 2 tbsp.

- Warm water 1 cup

- Salt 2 tsp.

Fillings

- Oil

- Pizza sauce ½ cup

- Diced green bell pepper, 1

- Shredded mozzarella cheese (Low-moisture), 1 cup

- Pepperoni 16 slices

- Sliced black olives (drained), 4oz can

Instructions

1. Make the dough: Stir together flour, salt, and yeast in a mixing bowl. Add water and oil. Mix the ingredients with the help of a spoon/fork till the dough forms. If it appears too wet, add more flour, then knead till a ball forms. Cover it and let it rise for 20 min.

2. Divide that dough into eight parts. Stretch n flatten that dough to roughly four and a half x 4 and a half-inch squares when working with the two pieces at a time.

3. Press the pie iron into the bottom plate with one square of the dough after oiling it. Load the following ingredients: 2tbsp. sauce, 1/4cup cheese, 1/4 bell pepper, 1oz olives, and 4pepperonis. Top it with the 2nd square of the dough. Close and lock pie iron.

4. Cook till the crust becomes golden brown; flipping is needed to assure even heat, over fire / on top of campfire embers. Depending on the campfire strength, the precise time would be different, but usually, this will probably take 2-3 min. Check it often.

5. Remove from heat, then unlock the pie iron thoroughly and turn out the pizza pocket.

6. With remaining ingredients, repeat. Be aware that while prepping subsequent pizza pockets, the iron would be HOT. Wait till the iron has been cooled / while reloading iron, take extreme caution.

Notes

Pre-Trip Prep: Dough can be prepared ahead of time at home and packed in your refrigerator in a container. To make it easy to roll out, remove it from the cooler 30 min before cooking.

Shortcuts: You can use pre-made, store-bought dough instead of producing your pizza dough.

10 Campfire Cheesesteaks

Prep time: 15 minutes, Cook time: 30 minutes, Serving 4, Difficulty: Normal

Per serving kcal: 278

Ingredients:

- Roast beef (1 pound-sliced)

- Salt and pepper (to taste)

- Onions (2)

- Loaf garlic bread (1)

- Green peppers (4)

- Vegetable oil (2 tbsp.)

- Pepper jack cheese (6 slices)

Instructions:

1. Slice the onion and green peppers into strips. (Before our camping trip, I do this at home and store it in a Ziplock bag.)

2. Heat oil over the fire in a skillet.

3. Add the onions and cook for 5 minutes or until they begin to brown until the oil is hot.

4. Apply the onions to the peppers and begin cooking until they are soft and tender.

5. Put on aluminum foil and cover with roast beef and open garlic bread.

6. After the onions and peppers have been cooked, put the roast beef on top.

7. On top of the onions and peppers, add all six slices of cheese.

8. Place the top slice on a sandwich of garlic bread and cover it with two foil layers.

9. Place over the fire or next to the coals and cook for around 10 minutes or until the cheese is melted.

10. Eat hot and break into four pieces

4.4 Desert

1. Churros Muffins

Prep time: 15min, cook time: 20min, Serving 24, Difficulty: Easy

Per serving: Calories: 89kcal, Fat: 4g, Net carb: 10.5g

Ingredients

Muffins:

- Butter melted 1/4cup

- White sugar 1/2cup

- Vanilla 1teaspoon

- Milk 1/2cup

- Salt 1/4teaspoon

- All-purpose flour 1cup

- Baking powder 1teaspoon

Churro Cinnamon Sugar Topping:

- Butter 1/4 cup

- Sugar 1/2 cup

- Cinnamon 1teaspoon

Instructions

1. Preheat the oven to 375 Fahrenheit. Coat a pan (24 mini-muffin) with the help of cooking spray.

2. Mix 1/4 cup butter & 1/2 cup sugar in a bowl. Whisk in the vanilla and milk, then whisk in the flour, salt, and baking powder until combined. Fill the muffin cups (prepared) about 1/2 full.

3. Bake in the oven until the muffins' tops are golden (lightly), for about 15 - 20 mins.

4. Place 1/4 cup of melted butter in a small bowl while the muffins are being baked. In a separate bowl, syndicate 1/2 cup of sugar & cinnamon.

5. Turn the muffin tin pan over to free the muffins on the cooling rack or plate.

6. Immerse all muffins individually in the butter, melted, and roll them in the mixture of sugar-cinnamon. Let them cool and serve.

2. Giant Oreo Skillet Cookie

Prep Time: 5 mins, Cook Time: 20 mins, Total Time: 25 mins, Serving 8, Difficulty: Easy

Calories per Serving: 708

Ingredients:

- Bag of Oreo cookies (14.3 ounces)

- Pre-made chocolate chip cookie tube (dough) (30 ounces)

Instructions:

1. Take your choice of Pillsbury cookie dough and press it into the cast iron skillet's bottom.

2. On top of the dough, chop up as many Oreos as you can fit.

3. Press the Oreo slightly through the cookie dough.

4. Bake for 17-20 minutes in a 350-degree BBQ, house oven (or trailer oven), watching it carefully to see when the cookie finally reaches a beautiful golden brown.

5. Refrigerate and enjoy.

3. Good Snack Mix

Prep Time: 10 min Cook Time: 45 min Serving: 7 Difficulty: Normal

Per serving Net carbs: 18g fiber: 2g Fat: 11g Protein: 30g Cal: 180

Ingredients:

- Worcestershire sauce 4 tsp.

- Melted butter 3 tbsp.

- Seasoned salt 1 tsp.

- Canola oil 1 tbsp.

- Corn Chex 2 cups.

- Garlic powder 1/2 tsp.

- Shredded wheat bite-sized 2 cups

- Salted cashews 1 to ½ cup

- Crispix 2 cups

Instructions:

- Oven preheated to 250 degrees. The first five ingredients are mixed, toss with cashews & cereals, and then cover equally. Spread into the skillet coated with the cooking spray.

- Cook for forty-five mins, mixing every fifteen minutes. Cool perfectly before saving it in the airtight jar.

4. Campfire Banana Boats

Prep Time: 5 min Cook Time: 10 min Serving: 1 Difficulty: Easy

Per serving kcal: 179

Ingredients:

Classic banana boat

- Milk chocolate 2 tbsp.

- Banana 1

- Cracker square 1 graham

- Marshmallows 8 mini

Instructions:

1. Take the banana & slice it down the center (along the concave edge) with the skin already. Not even all the way through, however, till the tip of the knife grazes the skin. Tear slightly apart from the peel & banana.

2. Into the middle of the banana, put the tiny marshmallows & chocolate

3. Cover the banana in foil. Please put it on a campfire or barbecue for around 10 minutes before the fillings have melted and the banana has cooked.

4. Unwrap the banana & season it with a smashed graham cracker.

5. Samoa S'mores

Prep Time: 5 mins, Cook Time: 5 mins, Total Time: 10 mins, Serving: 8, Difficulty: Easy

Per serving kcal: 194

Ingredients:

- Samoa cookies (Homemade)

- Marshmallows

Instructions:

1. Marshmallows toasting. By roasting them on an open fire, also you can microwave them for 8 to 10 secs on high, OR roasting them on a gas stove or over a grill, OR grilling them in the oven on a baking sheet for around 1 minute before they are golden brown (check carefully as they quickly burn).

2. Put one upside down Samoa cookie. On top of the cookie, put on top a toasted marshmallow. The marshmallow is topped with a separate cookie of Samoa (right side up) and push down softly between the cookies to squish the marshmallow.

COOKING CONVERSION CHART

Measurement

CUP	ONCES	MILLILITERS	TABLESPOONS
8 cup	64 oz	1895 ml	128
6 cup	48 oz	1420 ml	96
5 cup	40 oz	1180 ml	80
4 cup	32 oz	960 ml	64
2 cup	16 oz	480 ml	32
1 cup	8 oz	240 ml	16
3/4 cup	6 oz	177 ml	12
2/3 cup	5 oz	158 ml	11
1/2 cup	4 oz	118 ml	8
3/8 cup	3 oz	90 ml	6
1/3 cup	2.5 oz	79 ml	5.5
1/4 cup	2 oz	59 ml	4
1/8 cup	1 oz	30 ml	3
1/16 cup	1/2 oz	15 ml	1

Temperature

FAHRENHEIT	CELSIUS
100 °F	37 °C
150 °F	65 °C
200 °F	93 °C
250 °F	121 °C
300 °F	150 °C
325 °F	160 °C
350 °F	180 °C
375 °F	190 °C
400 °F	200 °C
425 °F	220 °C
450 °F	230 °C
500 °F	260 °C
525 °F	274 °C
550 °F	288 °C

Weight

IMPERIAL	METRIC
1/2 oz	15 g
1 oz	29 g
2 oz	57 g
3 oz	85 g
4 oz	113 g
5 oz	141 g
6 oz	170 g
8 oz	227 g
10 oz	283 g
12 oz	340 g
13 oz	369 g
14 oz	397 g
15 oz	425 g
1 lb	453 g

Conclusion

Modern life can render you feel run-down, alone, and detached from everyone you love, regardless of the moment. From reality, it is evident that camping is the perfect way to heal your ills, raise your confidence, and increase your relationships. This seems to be a simple fix.

Camping is a chilling and adventurous activity for many. It is also a learning experience to take risks, go outside, and discover the wildlife. Camping has been a peaceful activity for many years. If you are too busy in your daily life and not giving time to your family or friends then camping is the best solution to both enjoy and spend time together. This book is your perfect guide for camping and enjoying the scenic beauty of nature with all the essential gadgets.

Overall, we hope that this book can be a true companion for you as you plan all your future journeys and will lead you to have your own creative modifications that enable you to render food a joyful and unique part of the adventures from now on.

Printed in Great Britain
by Amazon